The Seventies

The Seventies

Photographs by the
Daily Mail

Mary Fogarty

This is a Parragon Book
First published in 2003

Parragon
Queen Street House
4 Queen Street
Bath, BA1 1HE, UK

Text © Parragon
All photographs © Associated Newspapers Archive

Produced by Atlantic Publishing

A catalogue record for this book is available from the British Library.
ISBN 0 75259 027 8

Printed in China

The Seventies

This was a decade of crazes and phases. There was Osmondmania, then Rollermania. After the glitz of Glam Rock came music with a harder edge. Out went sequins, in came safety pins as the Sex Pistols and The Clash took pop music by storm.

Kids went mad for space hoppers and chopper bikes. Digital watches, video recorders and calculators all hit the shops - and cost a small fortune. Mums and daughters wore hotpants - if they dared - while dads had to decide if it really was "a lot less bovver with a hover".

On the sporting front, Borg, Spitz and Korbut became household names, while Muhammad Ali continued to break records in the ring.

It was the decade of Watergate, Soweto and Three-Mile Island. Domestically, there was the oil crisis and the 3-day week; Britain went decimal and joined the EEC; the country elected its first woman prime minister, and even had a Minister for Drought.

From the momentous and the apocalyptic to the offbeat and the trivial, the photographs in this book, from the archives of the Daily Mail, chart the people, places and events that made up a memorable decade.

The Seventies

Pan's People

Above: Pan's People, the regular dancing team on TV's *Top of the Pops* in the early Seventies. From the left: Ruth Pearson, Dee Dee Wilde, Louise Clarke, Babs Lord, Cherry Gillespie, Andrea Rutherford.
Opposite: Pop group Slade, one of the early 'Glam Rock' groups in the Seventies who had a string of hits including 'Cum on Feel the Noize', 'Mama weer all crazee now' and 'Merry Christmas Everybody'. This photograph, taken in 1970, shows Noddy, Don, Dave and Jimmy in their pre-Glam Rock skinhead days which was the inner city fashion before Glam Rock.

Political faces

Above: Roy Jenkins, Chancellor of the Exchequer in 1970. He is seen with the Budget Box at the Treasury. Labour lost power to the Conservatives in the general election in June that year as Ted Heath was installed as Prime Minister. The result was totally unexpected as nearly all the opinion pollsters had forecast an easy Labour victory.

Opposite: Jeremy Thorpe, MP for Barnstaple in north Devon and leader of the Liberal Party in 1970. The Liberals won only six seats in the 1970 general election. However, in the 1974 election the Liberal party improved to 14 seats and held the balance of power in a hung parliament. Thorpe was charged with plotting to murder male model Norman Scott in one of the most high-profile court cases of the Seventies. He was eventually cleared of all charges in June 1979.

Fashionable faces

Above: Lulu and husband Bee Gee Maurice Gibb, who has just shaved off his beard for a part in a musical. The Bee Gees were well established in the Seventies but hit the heights of fame with the songs they wrote for the film *Saturday Night Fever*, released in 1977 starring John Travolta.
Opposite: Strong patterns in bold colours were the theme of mid-Seventies fashion – the model wears an Art Deco print shirt in two different patterns from Clobber, with a butterfly leather belt and cream and orange silk scarf.

Look of the early Seventies

Above: Actors Edward Woodward and Judi Dench together in Covent Garden for a rehearsal for the National Youth Theatre. Edward Woodward won fame for his portrayal of TV detective Callan, while Judi Dench was awarded an OBE in 1970 for her services to theatre.

Opposite: The peasant look was popular in the decade. This fashion student was proud that her mini smock dress and white 'Byron' shirt were made for under £2.

The skinhead generation

Above: The early Seventies saw the continuation of the skinhead fashion which had developed from the mods during the late Sixties. At first the look was defined by short hair - a feather cut often with a razor parting. The mods' parka was replaced by the Crombie overcoat. Here, girls perform their 'Skinhead Dance' at Epping Public Hall. The music they danced to was Jamaican ska and reggae. *Opposite*: Skinheads running through the streets of Brighton chanting in support of their football team, Chelsea.

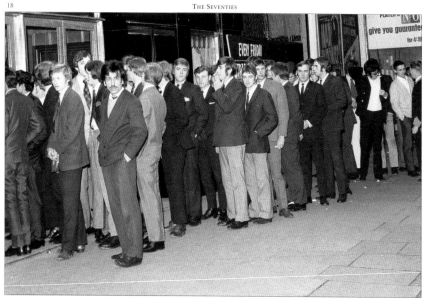

Preparing for the dance

Above: Australian singer Olivia Newton-John and American Ben Thomas rehearsing together.
Newton-John went on to star with John Travolta in the hit film *Grease* released in 1978.
Opposite: Two scenes from London's Hammersmith Palais. Men queued in droves on Friday nights
when the Palais began an experiment of making it the night the girls asked the men to dance.

Seventies symbols

Above: The Triumph Stag, the sports car that everyone wanted to own.

Below: The BAC Aerospatiale Concorde 001, which made its first flight in March 1969 but was not to come into commercial use until January 1976, with simultaneous take-offs from Paris to Rio de Janeiro and London to Bahrain. The Concorde seats 100 passengers and 3 flight crew and travels at a maximum speed of 1354 mph (2179 kph), which is 2.04 times the speed of sound.

Opposite: The Isle of Wight giant pop festival over the August Bank Holiday in 1970 attracted over a quarter of a million fans. The five-day festival enjoyed sweltering heat and many of the fans headed for the coast to cool off, chill out and let it all hang out.

The Parkinson show

TV presenter Michael Parkinson and actress Renny Lister, co-presenters of *Teabreak*, a magazine programme for housewives. Michael Parkinson became a household name in the Seventies,
presenting his own chat show in the late Saturday evening slot. It became an institution and attracted the world's leading celebrities from all walks of life. The show spawned a host of imitations but
often without the in-depth interviews that Parkinson managed to negotiate. The show was revived in
early part of the new century in its original format.
Opposite: A young dancer on *Top of the Pops* demonstrates the fashion of 1971: hot pants and thigh-
high boots.

The Jackson Five

Above: From Gary, Indiana, The Jackson Five, America's band of singing brothers hit fame in the early Seventies. They are from left to right: Marlon, Jackie, Tito, Jermaine and Michael, with 9-year-old Randy in a straw hat. At the age of 10 Michael Jackson became the youngest singer ever to top the charts. He led the vocals on 'I want You Back' which toppled Edison Lighthouse's 'Love Grows' from the number one spot. In 1970 the young pop stars spent 13 weeks at Number 1 in the US singles charts with their first four releases, selling over 15 million copies.

Opposite: The two girls pictured above were sent home from their school when they cut their hair in skinhead style. Their headmaster considered they had lowered school standards and banned them from school until their hair had grown back again. The fashion model below shows off her boot-laces: manufacture of shoelace braid quadrupled in 1971.

Band On The Run

Above: In 1971, while John Lennon released 'Imagine' and George Harrison had success with 'My Sweet Lord', Paul McCartney formed Wings with his wife Linda and Denny Laine. *Band On The Run* became one of the best-selling albums of the decade when it was released at Christmas 1973. It was McCartney's first critically acclaimed album since the Beatles and spent two years on both the UK and US charts selling over 6 million copies worldwide.

Opposite: Winkle pickers and stiletto heels stayed in fashion through much of the Seventies.

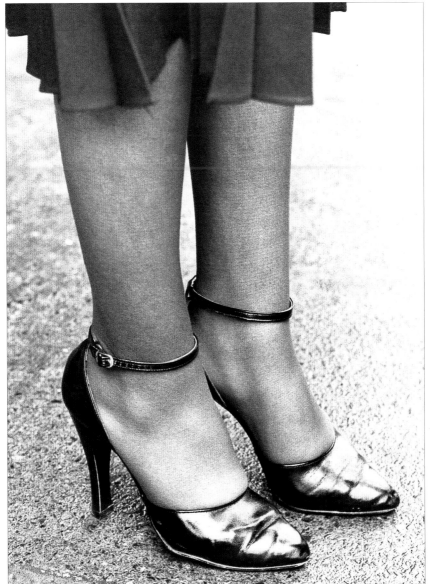

Football's worst and football's Best

Opposite: The Ibrox Park tragedy in 1971. 66 people were killed in Britain's worst soccer disaster to date at the end of a Rangers-Celtic match in Glasgow. Hundreds of spectators who were leaving turned back when they heard the roar of a Rangers goal and were caught under a mass of people still swarming down the steps. The disaster brought about compulsory safety licensing of all football grounds.

Above: George Best, still one of Manchester United's star players in the Seventies. Unfortunately his playboy lifestyle meant his career was not only marked by brilliant performances on the field but also by episodes of excessive drunkenness.

Imagine

Above: John Lennon and his wife Yoko Ono pose with Michael X on the roof of the Black Power headquarters. Both Lennon and Yoko spent most of the Seventies in New York fighting for peace and civil rights. In October 1971 Lennon released 'Imagine', his most successful and creative solo album. It contained a range of material from beautiful love songs to barely-veiled attacks on Paul McCartney.

Opposite: The miners' strikes of 1972 caused power cuts around the country. With no coal for the power stations blackouts lasting nine hours were imposed plunging Britain into darkness. The second series of strikes in 1974 was to bring down the Conservative government.

Miners' strike

Above: The miners' strike in 1972 saw trouble outside Saltley colliery, where miners had gathered in force to try to prevent lorries coming to collect coke. One driver rejected picket appeals to turn back and accelerated towards the depot gates. The crowd surged forward and Chief Inspector Shelley was crushed against the side of the lorry, losing consciousness and breaking his thigh.

Opposite: Wives sporting their husbands' helmets, marched on Westminster to protest on behalf of the miners.

The exhibition and the festival

Above: The Tutankhamun exhibition at the British Museum in 1972 was one of the most successful London had ever known, with long queues forming daily. Here the priceless gold mask of the young Egyptian king is unveiled for the first time. The 21in mask weighs 22.5 lbs and is inlaid with a jigsaw of cornelian, turquoise and lapis.

Opposite: Hippies at a summer rock festival.

Britain joins EEC

Above: Conservative Prime Minister Edward Heath. In January 1972 Heath signed the treaty admitting Britain into the Common Market. The new community of ten countries will have a population bigger than the United States. While this dominated political discussion at the time the familiar topics of the economy, wages, unemployment, industrial relations and inflation were all front-page news.

Opposite above: The famous chair from the TV series *Mastermind*, launched in the Seventies, with its Icelandic presenter, Magnus Magnusson, on the right.

Opposite below: Ronnie Wood, who would become a guitarist with the Rolling Stones in 1975.

The political scene

Above: Labour's Jim Callaghan out canvassing for votes. Callaghan was to become Foreign Secretary after the 1974 general election and went on to be Prime Minister in April 1976 after Harold Wilson surprisingly quit No 10. Callaghan beat off the challenge of both Denis Healey and Michael Foot in the leadership contest.

Opposite: The team from children's TV programme *Magpie*, ITV's equivalent of *Blue Peter* in the Seventies. Douglas Rae, Sue Stranks and Mick Robertson are decked out here in state-of-the-art fashion designed by Mr Freedom.

Rolling Stones romance

The inimitable Mick Jagger of the Rolling Stones and leading ladies' man and Bianca Jagger, the striking model from Nicaragua whom Jagger married in May 1971. A few years later they were divorced by which time Jagger faced a paternity suit from Marsha Hunt and had been cited in Marianne Faithfull's divorce proceedings. He finally took up with Bryan Ferry's Texan ex-girlfriend Jerry Hall.

Sporting moments

Above: David Bedford, Britain's 10,000-metre hopeful for the Munich Olympics in 1972. He went to the high altitudes in Kenya to prepare himself for the race. Bedford failed to win a medal but went on to break the world record for 10,000 metres on July 13 1973 with a time of 27 minutes 31 seconds.
Opposite: Liverpudlian boxer John Conteh had a successful career in the light-heavyweight division. This culminated in 1974 when he became the first British fighter to win the crown for 25 years by beating Argentinian Jorge Ahumada.

Fashion in the streets

Right: The maxi skirt was as fashionable as the mini skirt in the early Seventies. The model wears a black velvet skirt, with tartan taffeta cummerbund and white crepe pintucked blouse.

Opposite: Hot pants and platform shoes, all in silver and gold leather, designed by students at Kingston Poly School of Fashion.

Horror in Olympic village

Above: An Israeli athlete cries after the massacre at the Olympic Games in Munich, 1972. Nine members of the Israeli squad were killed, along with four of their Arab kidnappers from the Black September movement when a German police attempt to free the hostages went horribly wrong. A German policemen also died in the shoot-out.

Opposite: Simon Dee, TV's popular face in the Sixties and the early Seventies.

Northern Ireland

Above: Civil disturbances in Londonderry in 1972 brought British troops out onto the streets, culminating in 'Bloody Sunday', 30 January 1972, when 13 people were killed.

Opposite above: Troops and thousands of marchers proceed in silence in Dungiven after 'Bloody Sunday'. At first the soldiers barred the way with barbed wire, but after discussion allowed those bearing the white crosses (commemorating the dead) to place them on the steps of the RUC barracks.

Opposite below: Bernadette McAliskey (née Devlin) was a leading Catholic civil rights leader involved in many of the civil disturbances in northern Ireland in the early Seventies. At 21 she became a member of parliament for Northern Ireland.

Unlikely Heroes

Above: Bob Stokoe, the delighted manager of Sunderland football club, embraces his player Ian Porterfield, scorer of the winning goal against Leeds in the 1973 FA Cup Final. Stokoe was not known for such public displays of affection.

Opposite: Cyril Smith, the 27-stone Liberal MP for Rochdale, attempts to knit in a charity 'Knational Knit In' for arthritis and rheumatism. Well-known for his humour and appetite, Mr Smith was not, however, skilled on the domestic front.

Winning duo

Bobby Moore (left) and Sir Alf Ramsey (far right), captain and manager of the England football team in the 1966 and 1970 World Cup tournaments. Bobby Moore played for England's football team from 1962 to 1973, leading them to victory against West Germany in 1966. Moore saved some of his finest performances for the 1970 World Cup in Mexico when he was particularly outstanding in the match against Brazil. Controversy preceded the tournament when Moore was accused of stealing a gold bracelet, a charge on which he was later found innocent. Sir Alf continued to manage England until 1974 after England had failed to qualify for the 1974 World Cup.

Sporting moments

Above: Kevin Keegan, leading light for Liverpool Football Club in the Seventies, races to win the ball from Ken Burns of Birmingham in 1973, at the height of Liverpool's fortunes. Keegan appeared 230 times for Liverpool and scored 68 goals.

Opposite: Jackie Stewart, Britain's champion Formula One racing driver, celebrates victory winning the German Grand Prix in 1973. His five wins that year gave him his third driver's championship. It proved to be Stewart's last season in Formula One as a driver.

Previous page: Two of English football's most famous brothers – Jack and Bobby Charlton, who played for Leeds and Manchester United respectively.

Platforms were the go

The British Footwear Show in 1973. Platform heels were all the rage in the 70s, coming in all colours, shapes and sizes. Heel heights ranged from 2 to 5 inches, and platform heights from half an inch to 4 inches.

Teen idols

Donny Osmond, lead singer with The Osmonds pop group, and heart-throb for thousands of screaming fans in the UK. He had two big solo hits with 'Puppy Love' and 'Too Young' at the age of 15.

Opposite: Marc Bolan, who, with his band T Rex, was part of the 'Glam Rock' movement of the early Seventies. Bolan was the only artist to bridge the gap between the hippies of the Sixties and the new decade. In 1971 and 1972, T Rex were the best-selling singles band with hits like 'Metal Guru', 'Ride A White Swan' and 'Get it on'. Significantly, one of his concert tours in 1976 marked the change of times in the decade when he was supported by The Damned. Bolan was tragically killed when his car crashed at high speed into a tree in September 1977.

Shocking audiences

Above: The Seventies witnessed the 'streaker' phenomenon - characters who shed their clothes and 'streaked' in front of others in public places, sometimes just for dramatic effect, sometimes to make some kind of statement. Here a streaker takes off on a film set in London.

Opposite: Rock star David Bowie, seen here in his Ziggy Stardust guise, shocked his fans with the announcement in 1973 that he was to give no more concerts. Bowie's appearance - flame-red hair, vivid make-up, shimmering skintight Lurex suits on a razor-thin body and diamante platform boots - inspired a generation to dress like him.

Princess Anne marries

Above: Her Royal Highness Princess Anne with Mark Phillips at Buckingham Palace on the return from their wedding on November 14 1973. As the bride and groom were world-class riders there were many sporting friends among the 1500 guests at Westminster Abbey. Princess Anne had won a European gold medal while Mark Phillips had an Olympic gold.
Opposite: The happy couple on the balcony at Buckingham Palace and (below) returning from their wedding in Westminster Abbey.

Hunt 'the shunt'

Formula One world champion James Hunt marries his first wife, an ex-Miss World. Despite his playboy lifestyle, Hunt 'the shunt' - as he was affectionately nicknamed - won 10 Grands Prix between 1973 and 1979, driving for March, Hesketh and McLaren. 1976 was the pinnacle of his career when he won the drivers' championship in a McLaren by a margin of just one point from Niki Lauda.

Opposite: The Wallys of Wiltshire come to London in 1974 to do battle in court with the Department of the Environment, who wanted to evict them from their encampment half a mile away from the altar stone at Stonehenge. The Wallys were a group of hippies who all gave themselves the surname Wally.

Street fashion in London and Paris

Opposite: The mid-Seventies look from the Parisian flea market - chunky cardigan, long knitted scarf and baggy trousers.

Left: A more prosaic look on the streets of London. The midi skirt came in, with stripes for spring, and the inevitable platform soles.

When rock was young

Above: The fresh-faced David Cassidy, star of TV's *The Partridge Family* and singer of other artists'
songs, reduced thousands of screaming boppers to complete hysteria. One hit followed another -
'I Think I Love You' and 'How can I be sure' were but two - in the UK (he was less successful in the
States) and the fans couldn't get enough of him. David soon tired of being mobbed and employed
'strong arm men' to protect him on his public appearances.

Opposite: Elton John in one of his mock-Liberace, Crocodile Rock-style performances. Composer of
some of the 70s' best melodies, including 'Your Song', 'Candle in the Wind', 'Daniel' and 'Goodbye
Yellow Brick Road', Elton John achieved enormous international fame which was to continue for
three decades. Throughout the Seventies he was never out of the US album charts and in 1974,
tickets for his three Los Angeles shows sold out in minutes.

Travelling in style

The Ford Capri was modelled on the Ford Mustang but modified for the British market. Almost two million of these cars were sold in the Seventies. There were a number of modifications, but the car always retained the same distinctive sleek exterior and was popular until well into the Eighties. *Opposite*: Leaders of the three main political parties of the Seventies caught in a rare moment of unity, as they each place £1.00 in a silver rose-bowl for charity in 1974. From left to right: Edward Heath, (Conservative), Jeremy Thorpe (Liberal) and Harold Wilson (Labour).

Sporting heroes

Above: Bill Shankly, manager of Liverpool football team, after his farewell match. Shankly was Liverpool's much-loved manager for 15 years from 1959 to 1974, during which time he brought the team up from the lower half of the Second Division to heights of glory in the First Division. Amongst their many victories, the team won the UEFA Cup in 1972 and the FA Cup in 1974.
A statue to Shankley, with arms outstretched in the pose of the above photograph, stands proudly in front of Anfield's Kop end, reminding fans of his achievements at the club and the foundations he laid for future success.
Opposite: Joe Bugner engages in a mock bout with the legendary Muhammad Ali on the streets of New York. Joe Bugner's long career in boxing spanned three decades, peaking in the Seventies. He fought Ali twice - in 1973 and 1975 - but Ali won both times. Ali famously regained his world heavyweight title against George Foreman in the 1974 fight in Zaire dubbed 'The Rumble in The Jungle'.

Pouting lips and romance

Gravel-voiced Rod Stewart was as equally famous for his hit records as for his range of blondes. Here he is seen with girlfriend and actress Britt Ekland in 1975 shortly after they met at a Los Angeles party. She was later to become his wife.
Opposite: Mick Jagger, with the Rolling Stones, belts it out at Earls Court in 1973.

Glitter rock

David Bowie, rock idol of the Seventies, rides into town declaring that the country would benefit from a Fascist leadership and offering his own services. In 1975 Bowie went in a completely different direction when he filmed *The Man Who Fell to Earth* at Knebworth Park in Hertfordshire. By 1976 he had moved to Berlin, where he wrote *Heroes*, and became a near-recluse.

Opposite: Gary Glitter gives it his all during one of many 'poprock' spectaculars. Glitter's tight gold and silver shiny lamé bodysuits were as outrageous as his rather camp over-the-top performances of hits such as 'Do You Wanna Touch Me?'

The Goodies and TISWAS

Opposite: Today Is Saturday Wear A Smile: Chris Tarrant and Sally James, co-presenters of Seventies children's cult TV programme *Tiswas* which was watched by as many adults on a Saturday morning as children. Below them a *Tiswas* moment: Ian Lees, Chris Tarrant, John Gorman and Sylvester McCoy perform the 'Bucket of Water Song'. The show launched the career of Chris Tarrant and developed the profile of Lenny Henry who made regular appearances.

Above: Goody, goody yum yum... The Goodies, BBC's manic comedy team who presented a long-running series of slapstick, tricks and surreal storylines. Left to right: Bill Oddie, Graeme Garden and Tim Brooke-Taylor.

Hammers win the Cup

The FA Cup Final between Fulham and West Ham, Wembley 1975: Alan Taylor scores the second of his two goals for The Hammers in their 2-0 victory.

Opposite: West Ham's Trevor Brooking is mobbed by delighted fans at the end of the match. Below, wives and girlfriends of the West Ham team about to board the coach for Wembley.

Graham Hill killed in plane tragedy

An official examines the wreckage of the Piper Aztec in which Graham Hill and five others died. Hill was piloting the aircraft on its return from Marseilles, where he and his team had been testing a new car. The plane came down in thick fog on Arkley golf course just three miles from its destination, Elstree airfield.

Opposite: A model demonstrates a mid-Seventies 'pageboy' hairstyle.

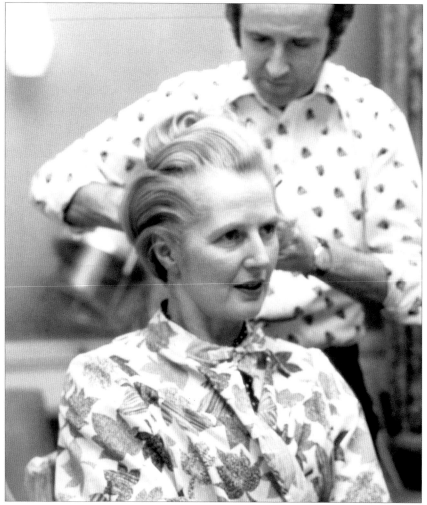

Hairstyles

Above: Britain's 'Iron Lady' of the Seventies, Margaret Thatcher, finds time to get her hair done, even though the battle for the Tory leadership had just begun between her and Edward Heath.
She apologised for her appearance: 'I must look a mess, but life's a bit difficult at the moment.'
Opposite: Hairstyles were decidedly more cropped than Thatcher's at the Lacy Lady disco in Ilford.

Wilson's shock resignation

Previous page: Harold Wilson leaves 10 Downing Street after his sensational resignation announcement in March 1976. The resignation came completely out of the blue, stunning his own Cabinet colleagues and politicians everywhere throughout Britain. He explained that, after his victory in 1974, he had decided he would only stay in office for two years and 'I have not wavered in this decision'.

Above: Batsman Murray for the famed West Indies cricket team is clean bowled by England's John Snow during the second day of the second Test at Lord's cricket ground in 1976.

Opposite: Olga Korbut, the diminutive Russian gymnast who stole the hearts of the crowd at the 1972 Munich Olympic Games, coming away with three gold medals. She returned to take another gold at the Montreal Olympics in 1976 but retired from the scene after this to become coach to the Soviet team.

Stars of the Centre Court

Above: The Centre Court at Wimbledon in 1977. Fiery Rumanian, Ilie Nastase, argues with the umpire while Swedish Bjorn Borg quietly sits it out. Borg went on to win the championship, something he was to achieve five times before he retired.

Opposite: American tennis star Chris Evert, also in 1977 - she won the Wimbledon championship three times in the Seventies and Eighties.

Mighty Liverpool win the European Cup

Emlyn Hughes, Liverpool's captain, holds the European Cup high in jubilation after the team's emphatic victory against the German side Borussia Monchengladbach with a score of 3-1.
Opposite: Kevin Keegan leaves Liverpool to join Hamburg. Keegan went on to win the coveted European Footballer of the Year in two consecutive seasons.

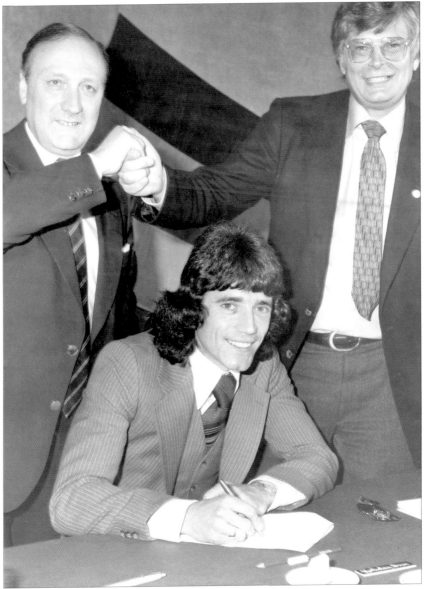

Silver Jubilee - the country rejoices

The official week of festivities for the Silver Jubilee in June 1977 began with the Queen lighting a giant bonfire in Windsor Great Park. It was the first of a hundred beacons all around the country that lit the skies. Everywhere people celebrated, holding street parties, and when she attended the thanksgiving service at St Paul's, over a million people lined the procession route. Wherever she went she was met with enthusiasm and great warmth. To mark the anniversary, she undertook an extensive tour of the world.

Above: The Queen and Prince Philip kneel in Westminster Abbey for the service.

The Grunwick dispute

Above: Miners' leader Arthur Scargill arriving at Grunwick in 1977 to lend his support to the picketers on their march. The public face of strikers in the Seventies, Scargill's appearance at any such event would always guarantee publicity. The Grunwick dispute was all about union recognition at the one factory, but Scargill and other unions carried out secondary picketing.
Opposite above: There was a heavy police presence at Grunwick: here police commissioner David McNee arrives to assess the situation.
Opposite Below: The scene in Willesden High Street after the pickets had clashed with police.

The coming of Punk

Above: The punk rock movement of the late Seventies was an aggressive, 'in-your-face' movement. Here punk rockers go mad in a Soho night club in 1977, swearing and spitting and smashing beer glasses.

Opposite: Denis Healey, Chancellor of the Exchequer, with his wife and some enthusiastic admirers on the Brighton seafront during the Labour Party Conference of 1977. Healey had earlier let slip that the Party had decided on a general election for the following autumn.

Punk rock

Above: Punk rockers on the King's Road in Chelsea. Punk rockers made a point of looking as rebellious and outlandish as possible. Their devil-may-care attitude often led to clashes with other groups.

Opposite: A punk rocker with one of the more exuberant hair styles at Piccadilly Circus.

Carter's 'Spirit of Camp David'

In September 1978 US President Carter was praised by world leaders for bringing together the two warring nations of Egypt and Israel at Camp David. The peace treaty was signed by Anwar Sadat and Menachem Begin. Begin said that Carter had 'worked harder than our forefathers did in Egypt building the pyramids'.

Above: President Carter walks up Whitehall to the Banqueting Hall, along with French President Giscard d'Estaing and Germany's Chancellor Helmut Schmidt.

Opposite: The punk models more 1977 punk rock fashion - the black leather jacket went well with a transparent pink luminous T-shirt.

Firemen go on strike.

Above: In November 1977 the firemen went on strike and 6000 of them marched on Downing Street. They took with them a petition with half a million signatures calling on Prime Minister Jim Callaghan to agree to their wage demands.

Opposite: Firemen picketing the fire station at Chelsea read messages of support.

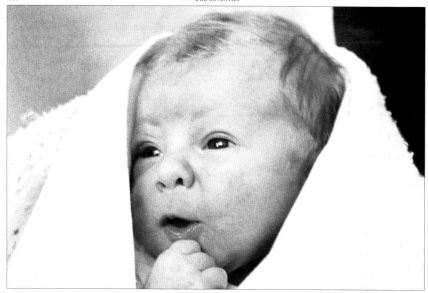

Hat-trick of wins for Borg

A happy Bjorn Borg holds up the Wimbledon singles trophy for the 3rd consecutive time in July 1978, having beaten Jimmy Connors in one of the greatest finals the tournament had ever seen. The last man to perform the feat was Fred Perry in 1934-5-6.

Opposite above: The world's first test-tube baby, Louise Brown, is born by a Caesarean operation at Oldham District General Hospital, July 1978. Patrick Steptoe, a pioneer of test-tube baby research, had spent more than 12 years perfecting the technique.

Below: Lesley and John, Louise's happy parents.

The Sweeney

John Thaw (left) played the role of Inspector Regan in TV's *The Sweeney*, a tough crime series featuring the Flying Squad at Scotland Yard. On his right his superior Haskins, played by Garfield Morgan. The series was one of the first to depict the policemen in a more 'realistic' role, showing them as hard-hitting, heavy drinkers.

Opposite: Spain's greatest golfer, Severiano Ballesteros, who went professional in 1974 at the age of 17. By 1978 he had won tournaments in five countries and was still only 20. He won his first British Open in 1979, becoming the youngest-ever winner of the tournament in the 20th century.

Bringing comic sunshine

Above: Eric Morecambe and Ernie Wise snapped with their wives en route to Switzerland, where they had been nominated for the Golden Rose of Montreux. Morecambe and Wise were one of Britain's most popular comedy teams in the Seventies, the highlight of each year being their Christmas show.

Opposite: A strange gathering of three top names from the Seventies but all with a love for sport. From left to right: Elton John, tennis star Billie Jean King, and rock star Rod Stewart.